J
)04
Lun

The Pomo Indians

by Bill Lund

Reading Consultant:
Clifford Trafzer, Ph.D.
Professor of Native American Studies
Director of Costo Historical and Linguistics
Native American Research Center

Bridgestone Books

an Imprint of Capstone Press

Bridgestone Books are published by Capstone Press
818 North Willow Street, Mankato, Minnesota 56001
Copyright © 1997 by Capstone Press
Printed in the United States of America

Library of Congress Cataloging-in-Publication Data
Lund, Bill, 1954-
    The Pomo Indians/by Bill Lund.
       p. cm.--(Native peoples)
    Includes bibliographical references and index.
    Summary: Provides an overview of the past and present lives of the
Pomo Indians, covering their daily life, customs, relations with the
government and others, and more.
    ISBN 1-56065-479-1
    1. Pomo Indians--Juvenile literature. [1. Pomo Indians.
2. Indians of North America--California.]   I. Title. II. Series:
Lund, Bill, 1954-   Native peoples.
E99.P65L86   1997
973'.049757--dc21
                                        96-39763
                                           CIP
                                           AC

Photo credits
Ben Klaffke, 8, 18
FPG/C.G. Randall, 20; Union Pacific Railroad, 16
Tommy Dodson, courtesy of Tom Renick, cover, 6, 10, 12, 14

Table of Contents

Map 4
Fast Facts 5
The Pomo Indians 7
Sweathouses and Acorns 9
The Pomo Family 11
The Shaman 13
Pomo Government 15
Pomo History 17
Famous Baskets 19
The Great Flood 21
Hands On: Guess the Stick 22
Words to Know 23
Read More 23
Useful Addresses 24
Internet Sites 24
Index 24

Map

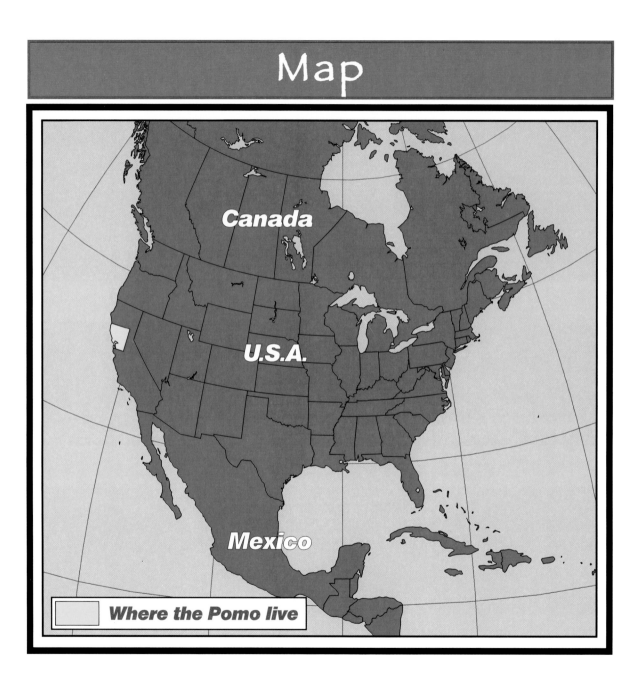

Canada

U.S.A.

Mexico

Where the Pomo live

Fast Facts

Today many Pomo Indians live like most other North Americans. In the past, they practiced a different way of life. Their food, homes, and clothes helped make them special. These facts tell how the Pomo once lived.

Food: The Pomo ate fish, nuts, and berries.

Home: They lived in round-topped houses made of reeds and grasses.

Clothing: Clothes were made of plants, bark, fibers, or threads. Men wore loincloths. A loincloth is a piece of cloth that passes between the legs. It is tied with a belt. Women wore skirts. Pomo also wore a piece of cloth called a mantle. The mantle was tied around the neck. It was belted at the waist. It protected the person from rainy or cold weather.

Language: There are seven major Pomo groups. Their languages are part of the Hokan language family.

Location: Pomo have always lived on land that stretched from the San Francisco Bay area north to Redding, California. They still live there today.

Special Events: Pomo have roundhouse dances and singing times throughout the year.

The Pomo Indians

Today between 4,000 and 5,000 Pomo Indians live in northern California. Once, more than 8,000 Pomo lived there.

Before European people came to California, the Pomo had a peaceful life. They hunted, fished, and gathered food from the forest. They used beads made from clamshells for money. They traded beads or supplies with other Pomo villages. Later, European settlers took most of the Pomo's land.

Today some Pomos live on a rancheria. A rancheria is land set aside for Pomo use. Each rancheria is governed by a group of elders. Elders are older, respected Pomo people.

Today many Pomo are learning about their past. Some are learning the Pomo language. Others are learning important songs and dances of the Pomo. In this way, they keep the old ways alive.

Many young people are keeping the old ways alive.

Sweathouses and Acorns

Today the Pomo live in homes like other North American people. In the past, they lived in round-topped houses. They made the houses with reeds and grass.

Each Pomo village also had a sweathouse. Inside, people poured water over hot stones to make steam. People took sweat baths every day. People also used the sweathouse to prepare for special days.

The Pomo used fish for food. They made strong boats out of reeds. They dried the fish they caught. That way they had food for winter.

Women and children gathered nuts, vegetables, and fruits. The acorn was an important Pomo food. They pounded acorns into powder. Then they used the powder to make bread and soup. The Pomo still eat foods made from acorns.

The Pomo used to live in reed and grass houses.

The Pomo Family

The family is very important to many Pomo. Family members live near one another. Sometimes they even live in the same house. Pomos have lived this way for hundreds of years.

Marriage and children are the most important parts of Pomo life. Grandparents still help raise children. They used to watch the children while the parents found food. Today grandparents watch children while parents work.

Pomo children start learning Pomo ways from birth. Some speak Pomo, tell old stories, and sing old songs. Some learn to make acorn mush.

In the past, girls learned more skills at age 12. They learned to make baskets and cook. Boys learned songs and how to hunt.

Today things are different. But some Pomo people travel to the ocean in the summer. They eat acorns and fish. They sing and dance.

Pomo children still learn special songs and dances.

The Shaman

Today some Pomo practice the same religion as other North Americans. A religion is a set of beliefs people follow. But other modern Pomo practice an old Pomo religion. They sing and dance in the old way.

Pomo people have special places. These are called prayer rocks. The Pomo believe these rocks have special powers. This is an old belief that has been passed down.

Dances have always been an important part of Pomo's religion. Pomos do roundhouse dances and have singing times. They believe dances bring power, good luck, and health.

In the past, a shaman was the head of Pomo religion. The shaman was the person in charge of religious events. The shaman was often a doctor, too. The shaman used herbs to cure patients. They also used special dances and songs to help heal the sick.

Pomos have special places called prayer rocks.

Pomo Government

The Pomo are divided into seven groups. Each group speaks a different dialect of the Hokan language. A dialect is the way a language is spoken. Dialects can change in different places or among groups of people.

Usually, one large family group made up each Pomo village. Sometimes more than one family lived in a village. They would form a ruling group. Group members were the leaders of each family.

Each village ruled itself. Sometimes villages banded together. Pomo villages banded together during wars. This made their army stronger.

They also banded together to trade, fish, hunt, and gather food. Villages held trading feasts. During these feasts, people traded, sang, and danced.

Pomo people still gather together to dance and sing.

Pomo History

Early Pomos met Spanish, English, and Russian sailors and traders. Russian fur traders built Fort Ross on Pomo land. Russians made Pomo people work in the trading post. Pomo also had to raise food for the Russians.

Spanish people started missions in California. A mission is built to teach people about Christian religions. Christianity is a religion based on the teaching of Christ.

The Spanish forced some Pomo into their missions. Spanish priests and soldiers made slaves of some Pomo. The Spanish believed they owned Pomo men, women, and children.

More European settlers came to Pomo areas. The Pomo lost much of their land. They were not allowed to live there or gather food.

Most Pomo refused to leave their homeland. Today most Pomo still live in California. Now some live on rancherias.

The Spanish forced some Pomo into their missions.

Famous Baskets

Pomo people are still famous for their baskets. Baskets are usually made by women.

Pomo women weave together branches, roots, and grass. Some baskets are plain. In the past, these were used to hold food or herbs.

Some baskets are fancy. Women decorate them with designs, feathers, and shells. Long ago, decorated baskets were worth a lot of money.

People keep decorated baskets as art. Sometimes baskets are sold or given as gifts. They are also used for special religious events.

Some young Pomo women still learn how to make baskets. They keep the Pomo art of basket making alive.

Pomo also make earrings. Men's earrings are made of wood. They are decorated with designs, beads, and feathers. Women's earrings are made of small bird bones.

Pomo people are famous for their baskets.

The Great Flood

Pomo people have special stories that are called legends. Sometimes legends explain things that happen in nature. Many Pomo stories are about a tricky animal named Coyote. The Pomo tell this story about Coyote causing a flood.

People were being mean to Coyote's two boys. Coyote became angry. He decided to set the world on fire. Coyote used bark to start the fire.

Spider came down from the sky. He rescued Coyote and Coyote's boys. He took them up to the sky.

When Coyote came back, everything had been burned. Coyote was thirsty. He drank water until he became sick. A shaman came and jumped on Coyote's belly. Water flowed out of Coyote's belly. The water covered the land. It caused a flood.

Water from Coyote's belly caused a flood.

Hands On: Guess the Stick

Pomo people enjoy many different games. One of their favorite games is this guessing game.

What You Need

8 popsicle sticks
Markers or crayons

What You Do

1. Choose one of your eight popsicle sticks.
2. Take your markers or crayons. Draw designs on the stick.
3. Pick up the rest of the popsicle sticks. Divide them between your two hands.
4. Pick up the designed stick. Hide it in with the other sticks. Make sure no one sees where you hide it.
5. Put your hands behind your back. Have the other players guess which hand holds the designed stick.
6. If someone guesses correctly, it is their turn to hide the popsicle stick.

Words to Know

legend (LEJ-uhnd)—a special story that explains things in nature

mission (MISH-uhn)—a church or place that is built to teach people about Christian religions

rancheria (RANCH-ur-ee-ah)—land set aside for use by Pomo people

shaman (SHAH-men)—doctor and leader of Pomo religion

sweathouse (SWET-houss)—a house heated with steam; Pomo used it to bathe and to prepare for some religious occasions.

Read More

Landau, Elaine. *The Pomo*. New York: Franklin Watts, 1994.

Worthylake, Mary M. *The Pomo*. Chicago: Children's Press, 1994.

Useful Addresses

National Museum of the American Indian
Smithsonian Institution
Washington, DC 20560

Ya-ka-ama Indian Education
6215 Eastside Road
Healdsburg, CA 95448

Internet Sites

Codetalk Home Page
http://www.codetalk.fed.us/home.html

Native American Indian
http://indy4.fdl.cc.mn.us/~isk/

Index

acorn, 9, 11
basket, 11, 19
beads, 7
California, 5, 7
Fort Ross, 17
Hokan, 5, 15
legend, 21
loincloth, 5

mantle, 5
mission, 17
prayer rocks, 13
rancheria, 7
roundhouse, 13
shaman, 13
sweathouse, 9
village, 7, 15